THE ANCIENT HOUSES OF EGYPT

HOW JOSEPH BROUGHT THE ISRAELITES TO EGYPT, AND HOW MOSES DELIVERED THEM

JAMES TAIWO

INTRODUCTION

A prophecy was given years ago to a great man of God named Abraham about the Bondage, which was to come upon a certain generation and last 400 years. The prophecy was recorded in the great book that contains all truth, all records of things past and things that have not yet been seen but have been heard of by many.

Day after day, month after month, and year after year, what was said went into a sea of forgotten things. Men forgot about the days of pain to come. The dark cloud of fulfillment gathered up in the sky; things were beginning to fall, bit by bit, according to the prophecy. The plaintive music of the chains of slavery jingled like warning bells, yet both young and old danced to it like a Christmas carol.

The door opened unto them without anyone forcing it to do so. They thought they had found comfort and freedom from all suffering, pain and affliction, but just as is true with the road leading to hell, the horror that awaits at the end of the journey is never obvious to travelers.

They saw no evil coming their way, nor any wrong in their decision to move to the land they had been forewarned about; they chose to stay and, like the entrance of a prison, their opportunity to heed the prophecy clanged closed with iron bars. The bright, shining days of happiness became the dark nights of sorrow, and the alluring gold land became nothing but sand. All fate was lost to the horror, with no hope of the doors opening to them again.

TALES OF JOSEPH

There was a gifted man named Joseph, who was born into the family of Jacob and Rachael, the second to their youngest, Benjamin. Joseph was unique. His abilities brought upon him something he never conceived of: the hatred of his brothers. The seventeen-year-old boy was out in the fields with his brothers on the fateful day when he observed the evil that had crept into their family.

Dan, Naphtali, Gad, Asher, Judah, Reuben, Levi and Benjamin stood, the tall wheatgrass whispering around their robes, talking about Joseph and the love their father had for him.

. . .

2

Reuben: *What do you think of how our father has been treating Joseph?*

Judah: *It is obvious he loves him more than he loves the rest of us.*

Benjamin: *I do not really think so. He is just attached to him in a funny way, more than he is to us.*

Levi: *Shut up, Ben! Sometimes I wonder if you are for us or against us. You tend to say more good of him than bad. It must be because you are from the same mother.*

Benjamin: *It is not what you think. I noticed the love, too, but I just feel it is normal for parents.*

Joseph stood a distance from them, but he could hear what they were saying and felt it was wrong. They should have been cheerfully feeding the flocks! He decided he was going to tell his father about their discussion. Reuben made his way over to Joseph.

Reuben: *Hey! It is time to go home. Round it up already.*

Joseph: *All right, Reuben, I am already done.*

The brothers arrived home after trekking some distance.

Joseph: *Papa, I am home!*

Jacob: *My son, welcome home! I have a surprise for you!*

Reuben: *(to his other brothers) There goes father and son trying to make us jealous. Hey! Judah, hurry up with that stuff and let us go for dinner.*

Joseph: *(excited) Really? What is it?*

Jacob went into the house and came back with a very beautiful coat made of many colors.

Jacob: *This is for you, my son.*

Joseph shrieked in happiness and surprise.

Joseph: *Thank you very much papa! I love it!*

Dan: What!? He has never even given me a shirt before. Why I am not getting Papa's love like him?

Joseph's happiness faded a bit when he thinks of what he witnessed in the fields.

Joseph: Papa, I do not think my brothers love me. They were talking about you loving me more than you love them and they did not even do anything in the fields. They were just talking all day.

Jacob: It is not what you think, my son. They love you, and soon enough, you will realize it.

Joseph: But, Papa!

Jacob: No, my son, they love you and that is the truth.

Dinner was served and the wives called out to Jacob so that they could all eat together as one family. After, they relaxed and said their evening prayers together before going to bed.

Joseph: (in his room) Whoa! It has been a long day; I need to rest my bones.

He fell on his bed and off to sleep.

Just few minutes after closing his eyes, he was taken away in the dark. He awakened in a new world, the world of dreams. Joseph saw something amazing in his dream; he was out with his brothers, binding sheaves in the fields when his own sheaf arose and stood upright, and the sheaves of his brothers came around and made obeisance to his own sheaf.

Joseph woke in the morning and was just too happy to keep his dream to himself. His brethren were outside the house, preparing to go to the fields with their flocks to feed them.

Joseph: Wait! Wait! Wait! I have to tell you something about what I saw in my dream last night.

Dan: Go on, we are listening.

Reuben: *Yes, by all means, go on.*

Joseph: *I dreamt about something fantastic, we were together in the fields binding sheaves and my own sheaf suddenly rose up and stood upright and yours came around and made obeisance to my sheaf.*

Judah: *Wait! Wait! Wait! Dreamer boy, what exactly are you trying to say? Are you saying we all are going to worship you?*

Reuben: *Are you trying to say you will rule over us?*

Naphtali: *What is wrong with you, dreamer boy? You want to put us under your feet?*

Dan: *Get out of our sight!*

Levi: *I can't believe this nonsense is coming out of your mouth.*

Gad: *Please! Just get out, it is too early for this upset!*

Asher: *I am going. Listening to this in the morning is bad luck, very bad luck.*

Joseph stood, disappointed and immobilized, like a bird whose feathers are drenched with water. The brothers moved away, discussing how he would never stop amazing them with his nonsense and how they hated him even more.

JOSEPH WAS SOLD TO SLAVERY

The hatred Joseph's brothers had for him grew each time they saw him. The sight of him filled them with irritation.

In the dark of the night, Joseph was in bed when he was taken away again into the dream world. He saw something unusual again in his dreams. The sun, the moon and eleven stars were making obeisance to him. He woke up, sat on the bed and thought to himself, I do not know if it is the right thing to do, but I must tell my father, mother and brethren about it.

The family gathered at Joseph's request.

Joseph: I have something to say.

Dan: It had better be something reasonable this time around.

Jacob: Go on, my son.

Levi: (whispering in Naphtali's ear) I am certain it is another dream.

Joseph: I had a dream last night.

Naphtali and Levi gave each other knowing looks..

Joseph: In my dream, I saw the sun, the moon and eleven stars making obeisance to me.

Jacob: Keep quiet! I will not have you carry such a belief that we will worship you! What is this dream that you have dreamt? Never will it come to pass that your brother, mother, or I will worship you.

Zilpah: I told you the boy is up to some misfortune. Can you now see it for yourself?

Levi: He wishes we could all be his slaves!

Dan: Joseph! Can you dream about something else for once, so we could all smile without worrying?

Joseph looked at him in surprise.

Benjamin: It is just a dream! Why are you all taking it so seriously?

Jacob: Enough! You can all go and carry out your daily duties.

Benjamin and Joseph stayed behind at home while the others left for the fields to feed the flocks in Shechem.

Joseph and Benjamin went into the house talking to each other.

Six hours passed.

Jacob: Joseph! Joseph! Joseph!

Joseph: I am coming, Papa. Joseph rushed to his side. Here I am.

Jacob: Your brothers have been out on the fields at Shechem for a while feeding their flocks, and there has been no word from them since they left this morning. They should have come home by now. Please, I pray you, go and see if all is well with them and bring me word of them.

Joseph: As you say, Papa. I will be on my way.

Joseph departed from the house, heading to Shechem to find his brothers. He journeyed many miles, but he could not find them. He began to wander around about the place until a man noticed he was in trouble.

Man: Boy! That is a nice coat you have on you. Why are you looking so confused? Did you lose something?

Joseph: I am looking for my brothers; they came out here to feed the flocks, and we have not gotten any word from them, neither have they returned home. Please, have you seen them?

Man: Yes, they left this place for Dothan. Come, let us go to Dothan together. You should find your brethren there.

They headed toward Dothan with the hope of finding Joseph's brothers there. The journey was fruitful, as he found his brothers, but they caught sight of him before he got to them.

Reuben: Hey! Brothers, come. Is that not Joseph? I recognize his coat.

Levi: That is definitely Joseph.

Dan: Behold! The dreamer is coming!

The brothers laughed together in derision.

Judah: I suppose he has some negative news for us that he heard in his dreams. However, perhaps we could paint him in a negative light to our father.... Yessss, we can make him bad news to bring to our father. This is our opportunity! Let us kill him.

Levi: Yessss! We will cast him into the pit after slaying him.

The sibilant fervor in the brothers' cruel voices intensified.

Gad: We will tell our father he was killed by a wild beast!

Naphtali: Yessss! let him see how we will bow to him if he is dead! We will tell Father an evil beast did it. We will tell him we tried, but we were no match for the beast.

Gad: Yessss! Let him go to the grave with all his dreams…

Reuben jumped into the discussion when he heard they were considering, as their best option, killing their brother Joseph.

Reuben: Brothers! Let us not do this. We should not have blood on our hands, at least not the blood of our own brother. Let us cast him into a pit in the wilderness. He will not survive this. I am certain he will die with his dreams in a pit with no food or water.

Reuben actually had a plan to deliver him back to his father, because he does not want to break his father's heart.

The brothers yielded to Reuben's advice.

When Joseph got to his brothers, they did not even give him the opportunity to say anything before laying hold of him, stripping him of his coat of many colors and casting him into an empty pit in the wilderness. Reuben had left them to continue with the feeding of the flocks.

The brothers were sitting around eating bread when they noticed some Ishmaelites coming from the direction of Gilead, with their camels bearing spicery, balms and myrrh. They were heading down to Egypt.

Judah thought to himself that it would be wise to make some money from their disposal of their brother rather than killing him and having his blood on their hands.

Judah: Hey, everyone, behold the Ishmaelites coming in our direction. Let us make some money and sell Joseph, rather that stain our hands with his blood.

Levi: That is not a bad idea; let us wait until they get to us so we can see if they will buy him.

Naphtal: We have to pull him up before they get to this place.

They pulled Joseph, who was already weak and tired, out of the pit and waited for the arrival of the merchants.

Judah: Good afternoon, gentlemen.

Merchant 1: Good afternoon, what can we do for you?

Merchant 2: I suppose they have some bounty for sale, hmmm?

Judah: We have a business proposal for you. This man here is for sale as a slave. Are you interested in buying him?

Merchant 1: How many silver is he worth?

Judah and his brothers quickly and quietly talked to each other about how much they should sell Joseph for.

Judah: Thirty pieces of silver would do.

The merchants spoke to one another about the offer.

Merchant 1: We have only eighteen pieces to offer.

Judah: That is too low. Try to make it twenty-five.

Merchant 1: We cannot offer that much for him. Let us make it twenty.

Judah spoke with his brethren again and they agreed the price was fair enough.

Judah: We have a deal, then. You can have him.

The merchants gave them twenty pieces of silver and took Joseph to Egypt as a slave.

Later, Reuben went to check for Joseph in the pit, so he could pull him out of it.

Reuben: Joseph! Joseph! Where are you?

Reuben could not find him; he tore at his clothes and returned to his brothers in shock.

Reuben: The child is not in the pit anymore! Where has he gone! What has become of him?

Reuben asked many questions but got no answer from his brothers. They pretended, instead, to be confused about the situation.

Judah: Seeing that the boy is nowhere to be found, how do we explain the situation to our father? We have to think of a solution before we can go back home.

Asher: I think the best way is to make it seem like an evil beast killed him.

Gad: How do you suggest we do that?

Asher: Let us tears his coat, kill a sheep and soak the coat in the blood of the sheep. We will give this to our father as evidence to save our heads.

Judah: Let us hurry with it, then.

They brought forth a sheep, killed it, and soaked Joseph's coat of many colors in it. They returned home to their father even as Joseph was being pushed along the dusty road to Egypt to begin his new life. His life as a slave.

When they arrived home without Joseph, they wore varied masks of sadness. Benjamin came out of the house to greet them with an unusual look on his face. He was thinking of many things at once, but he never said a word.

Jacob: Welcome, my sons! Where is Joseph? I sent him to come looking for you. Where is my son?

They bowed their faces to the earth and could not say anything about his location.

Jacob: Reuben! What happened to your clothes? Why are you scraped and torn?

Judah then brought out Joseph's coat, soaked in blood, and gave it to his father.

Judah: Father! See if that is your son's coat.

Jacob held the coat with tears running down his cheeks, while Benjamin ranted, out of control, mad with grief.

Jacob: It is ... it belongs to my son. It belongs to Joseph.

He fell to the dust, his tears making mud.

Judah: We found it on our way back home.

Jacob: An evil beast has devoured my son! He is no doubt in pieces.

Jacob tore his clothes and put a sackcloth upon his loins. He mourned his son and refused to be consoled but vowed to mourn him even after his own death.

JOSEPH IN POTIPHAR'S HOUSE

The Midianites arrived at Egypt with Joseph and sold him out to Potiphar, who was captain of the guard of Pharaoh and an Egyptian.

Merchant 1: Sir, we have a boy for sale.

Potiphar: Where is he?

They brought Joseph to him and he found favor in the sight of Potiphar, who bought him and took him to his home in Egypt.

Potiphar: Boy! What is your name?

Joseph: I am Joseph.

Potiphar: Good name! This is my place, and this is where you will be staying. Do you have energy and are you hard working?

Joseph: Yes, sir.

Potiphar: Let me show you your room.

Potiphar called his wife to tell her about the new boy. His wife liked him and welcomed him into the house, but her liking of him seemed to be more than what a wife should have for a slave.

Potiphar's wife: Come, let us go to your room.

The life of Joseph as a slave in the house of Potiphar began from that moment and brought unexpected increase to the house and everything around them, because Joseph carried the presence of God within him. One day, Potiphar called Joseph.

Potiphar: Joseph! Joseph!

Joseph: Yes, master!

Potiphar: Come, sit beside me, let us have a drink together.

Joseph sat with his master and they got to talking.

Potiphar: Your presence in my house has brought unexpected increase, and I have decided to reward you for that. I am going to make you the head over everything in my house.

Joseph was excited and could not find a better way to express his happiness than by breaking into tears as he said thank you to Potiphar, his master. The house of Potiphar experienced more increase and prosperity from that moment but, as is too often the case, something happened that changed everything.

Potiphar's wife: Joseph! I would like you to help me get some things from the store and bring them to my room.

Joseph: As you say, mistress.

Joseph did as the master's wife wanted him to without question or hesitation. She would wake Joseph up or make him stop what he was doing to do things for her at ridiculous hours of the day and night. She would move very close to him whenever they were talking. Joseph felt uncomfortable about this sometimes, but he did not do anything about it, as she was the wife of his master.

Potiphar: Joseph! I will be traveling on an assignment tomorrow, and I want you to take good care of the house, as you always do.

Joseph: Yes, master, I will. Your home is safe with me.

Potiphar's wife seemed to be excited about the journey of her husband, but Joseph paid her no attention. Joseph left the presence of his master to attend to his many duties.

Potiphar's wife: You really trust this boy. Are you certain he can handle all the responsibilities given to him?

Potiphar: I trust him. He can.

The next day, Potiphar went on his journey, leaving everything in Joseph's care. A few hours later, the wife called Joseph.

Potiphar's wife: Joseph! Come.

Joseph: Yes, mistress. Here I am. What is your will?

Potiphar's wife: Come closer to me. Joseph! Do you know you are supposed to be taking care of me? Didn't your master tell you to take care of everything in his absence?

Joseph: I am taking good care of you, mistress. What would you have me do to make you comfortable?

Potiphar's wife: Do you know I really love you, and I want us to be together? See that your master is not about; we can have an affair together and keep it between ourselves.

Joseph: Never! I cannot be with you, because my master has not given you to me.

Joseph extricated himself from her embrace and left the chamber before she could grab hold of him again.

The next day, she tried to seduce Joseph by dressing provocatively, but Joseph was able to resist her.

Two days later, she called Joseph to come and see her.

Potiphar's wife: Joseph! I want you in my room now; I want you to fix something for me.

Joseph: I am on my way, mistress.

Potiphar's wife: Over there—I think something is wrong with the bed. Please check if you can fix it for me.

She undressed herself, remaining in just her underclothes. She held him from behind, caressing him with her hands. Joseph turned around, for all his innocence still knowing what she was about. He tried to run from the room, but she held his tunic, preventing him from fleeing. Joseph quickly removed the garment and fled from the room without it.

Knowing it could lead to trouble, Potiphar's wife cried out to the men of the house.

Man 1: What has happened?

Man 2: Is everything as it should be?

Potiphar's wife began to wail.

Potiphar's wife: Look, he has brought in a Hebrew boy to mock us. He tried to force himself on me. I fought with him so hard, and when I lifted my voice to call out to people in the house, he left his garment and fled from the room.

Man 1: What?!

Man 2: How could Joseph have done this thing?

They left their master's wife and headed back to their post.

Potiphar's wife kept the garment beside her, as she knew her husband would be back soon.

Potiphar returned home to hear his wife's weeping.

Potiphar: What!? Why are you crying? What has happened? Where is Joseph?

Potiphar's wife: Joseph! Please do not bring that boy close to me again. The Hebrew boy did this to me. He came to my room and tried to force himself on me, but I resisted him and tried to cry out to the men of the house before he ran away from the room, leaving his tunic behind.

Potiphar: After everything I have done for this boy, he has decided to repay me with evil? Joseph! Joseph!

Potiphar got hold of Joseph and, without waiting for an explanation, he cast the boy into the king's prison. In a matter of moments, Joseph fell from the level of a leader to that of a prisoner.

~

The Prison

Some of the prisoners surrounded Joseph, curious.

Prisoner 1: What brought you to this place? Is Potiphar not your master?

Prisoner 2: I have heard news about the good things you did in his place. How come he is putting you in prison?

Prisoner 3: Maybe it has gone badly.

Some other prisoners laughed when they heard about Joseph, but no one treated him badly for any reason.

Potiphar went home without Joseph, and his wife was very happy about it.

Potiphar's wife: *Make sure he does not get out of that prison.*

Potiphar: *Worry not, wife. He will remain there for the rest of his life.*

The presence of God never left Joseph, and everything he laid his hands upon in the prison prospered. One day, the warden addressed Joseph.

Prison keeper: *Your good behavior amazes me. I do not really care what brought you here, and I think I can make good use of you when the time comes.*

THE DREAM COMES TRUE: THE PRISONER BECOMES THE RULER

After two weeks, Potiphar had completely forsaken Joseph, making no effort to get him out of prison.

Prison Keeper: Joseph! I have found you to be a good man, so I am putting you in charge of all the affairs of the prison and all the prisoners in it.

Some weeks after making Joseph the ruler of the prison, a butler and a baker at the royal palace are brought before Pharaoh.

Pharaoh: Bring me the two of them!

Pharaoh's guard: Yes, your royal majesty.

Pharaoh: For the sins you have committed, I cannot let you go without any punishment. Guards! Cast them into the prison.

The guards took them and cast them into the prison according to Pharaoh's command.

Days later, they both had a terrible and frightful dream.

Butler: Ooh! What sort of dream is this?

Baker: You also had a dream?

Butler: Yes!

Baker: I likewise did, but this is a prison. We cannot get anyone to interpret for us.

Joseph: Gentlemen, interpretation is of the Lord. Tell me your dreams; I can tell you their meaning.

Butler: Hebrew boy! How can you do that?

Joseph: Just tell them to me.

Butler: In one dream, a vine was before me. It had three branches; it budded and its blossoms shot forth and the clusters thereof brought forth ripe grapes, and pharaoh's cup was in my hand. I took the grapes, and pressed them into Pharaoh's cup, and I gave the cup to Pharaoh.

Joseph: This is the meaning of your dream: in three days, Pharaoh shall remember you and deliver you from the prison, and you shall serve him the same way you always did serve him.

Butler: Could this be true?!

Joseph: Forget me not, when it is well with you.

Baker: This is amazing. Tell me the meaning of my dream and I shall pay you. I saw three white baskets on my head and, in the uppermost, there were all manner of meat for Pharaoh and the bird did eat of them out of the basket upon my head.

Joseph: This is the meaning of your dream: within three days, Pharaoh shall also remember you, but he shall lift off your head from your neck and put you on a tree, and birds from the sky shall eat thy flesh from thee.

The baker was terrified to hear about the tragedy that would fall upon him, but he did not ask for a solution to escape his fate.

The events occurred according to Joseph's interpretations. The butler was delivered in three days' time, and he was restored to the house of Pharaoh. He forgot about Joseph, though, and said nothing of him until two years had passed and Pharaoh had a dream that troubled his heart. He woke up in the morning with great worries.

Pharaoh: What sort of dream was this? Guard! Get me the magicians.

Guard: Yes, your highness.

When the magicians arrived, Pharaoh came out and narrated his dream to them.

Pharaoh: I had a dream and behold, there came out of the river seven well-favored kine, and fat-fleshed they were, and they fed in the meadow. However, seven other kine came up of the river, ill-favored and lean-fleshed, and they stood by the well-favored, fat kine, and I woke up. I went back to my sleep, and I beheld in my dreams seven ears of corn come up upon one good stalk, and seven thin ears blasted when the east wind sprung up after them. The seven thin ears devoured the seven full ears. What is the meaning of these dreams of mine?

Magician 1: Your highness, this goes beyond our skill to tell.

Magician 2: Never has such a strange dream been heard of during the reign of any king.

Pharaoh: So! You all have no answers for the mystery before me? Depart from me, then, for I have no use of you.

Pharaoh retreated into his room, and the butler heard of the issue and remembered Joseph. He hurried to tell Pharaoh that he had a solution to his problem.

Butler: *Your excellency, I know of someone who can interpret your dreams.*

Pharaoh: *Who is that person?*

Butler: *His name is Joseph. He is a Hebrew. I was with him in the prison, and he interpreted my dream and the dream of the baker and all happened according to what he told us.*

Pharaoh: *Is that true? Get him at once.*

The guards departed to get Joseph.

Pharaoh: *Boy! I was told you can interpret my dreams.*

Joseph: *With God by my side, I can.*

Pharaoh: *Hear thee my dreams then.*

Pharaoh related the dreams to Joseph.

Joseph: *Sir, both dreams are one. God has revealed to you things to come. The seven good kine are seven years, as are the seven good ears of corn. The seven thin and ill-favored kine that came up after them are seven years, as are the seven empty ears blasted with the east wind.*

There shall be seven years of plenty in the land, and there shall be seven years of great famine in the land. But let Pharaoh choose for himself a wise man, let him set the man over the affairs of Egypt and let the man store food from the years of abundance and save it for the years of famine to come.

Pharaoh sat and pondered what to do concerning what God had revealed to Joseph.

Pharaoh: *Joseph! Since God has shown that to you which my magicians could not reveal, there is no other so discrete and wise as you in the land. I therefore appoint you the head over my house and the land of Egypt. Only in the throne will I be greater than you. Stretch forth your hand. This is my ring, a symbol of the authority I have given to you.*

Pharaoh also clothed him with fine linen, put a gold chain about his neck, and made him ride on his second chariot, and the people of the land bowed and kneeled before him. Joseph became a top authority in the land, and no decision could be made without his consent. He was named Zaphnathpaaneh and given a wife named Asenath, who was the daughter of the priest, Potipherah.

After seven years of abundance, the years of famine were upon the land, but Joseph had done all that was necessary to keep the land safe and the people and animals from starving. He and Asenath were likewise plentiful, bringing forth two children in the land of Egypt: Manasseh and Ephraim.

When the famine began to take hold, people gathered in front of Pharaoh's palace complaining about the lack of food.

Pharaoh: People, why do you complain about food? Go to Joseph. Whatever he tells you to do, do it.

Muttering and complaining, they left to see Joseph.

Joseph: Please, good people; there is enough food for everybody.

Joseph opened the stores and gave out food to the people, and they were well satisfied. The famine grew great far across the region, and the house of Jacob was affected. Egypt became the only land with abundant food that people could buy, so Jacob told his sons to journey to Egypt to get some corn. Ten of Joseph's brothers, excluding Benjamin, packed and journeyed to Egypt to do their father's bidding.

Joseph: You! Supply those people there with corn. And make sure nobody breaks the line!

Reuben: Good day, sir!

Reuben bowed before Joseph along with his brethren, and when they lifted their faces up, Joseph recognized them. They knew him not, and Joseph remembered his dreams.

Joseph: Why have you come? Ye are spies sent to see the nakedness of the land.

Brothers: No, sir!

Judah: We have only come to buy food.

Reuben: We all are the sons of one man.

Joseph: No! You are spies sent to see the nakedness of the land!

They all responded "No" again.

Judah: Thy servants are twelve, but the youngest is at home with our father.

Joseph: That proves you are spies from another land and, because of this, you shall not leave unless your youngest brother comes around. Guards! Put them in the ward.

Three days later, Joseph came, along with his interpreter.

Joseph: I have decided to make your punishment light. If you are truthful with your claims, let one of you stay behind while others go and come back with your youngest brother.

Joseph wanted to be sure that the same fate that had befallen him at the hands of his brothers did not also fall upon Benjamin. The brothers huddled to communicate with each other in Hebrew tongue.

Judah: We are all guilty of killing our brother.

Dan: He begged us, but we did not listen.

Reuben: Did I not beg you not to spill the blood of the lad? Now his blood is required of us.

Because Joseph could hear everything, he became emotional and turned away from them so they would not see his welling eyes.

Joseph: You! Simeon! You are staying back. Guards! Fill their bags with corn and let them go.

Joseph bound Simeon before them. The brothers departed from Egypt. On the way, Asher opened his sack to check the corn and found his money has been restored to him.

Asher: What? Look, my money is restored to me.

They walked in fear as they journeyed back to their father's house.

Jacob: Welcome home, my sons. Is everyone well?

Reuben: The man who is the lord of the land spoke to us roughly took us as spies of the country.

Judah: He kept us captive, but we pleaded with him that we are true men and not spies. He decided to release us on the condition that one person stay behind till we come back with our youngest brother.

Levi: He took Simeon.

Levi open his sack and his bag of money fell out.

Levi: My money was restored, too.

Dan: Mine is also in my sack.

They all emptied their sacks and found out everyone's money was included in his sack. They became more afraid.

Jacob: You have bereaved me, my remaining sons, by losing your brothers. Joseph is not, Simeon is not, and now you want to take Benjamin from me?

Reuben: Please! Let Benjamin go with us. I promise I will bring him back to you. If I fail, slay my two sons.

Jacob: No! He will not go with you. His brother is dead and he is alone. If something should happen to him, I will die a sorrowful old man.

They pleaded with Jacob to release Benjamin, but he refused to let him go. They could not return to Egypt without him, and the famine grew worse. Their animals were skin and bones, as were the people; the stores of corn were exhausted.

Jacob: Reuben! Call your brothers and go to Egypt to get corn, lest we all starve.

They gathered once again to make the journey to Egypt.

Judah: The man we saw made an official decree that we would not see his face until we bring our brother Benjamin to him. We will go to Egypt to get corn only if you agree to send our brother with us.

Jacob thought in sorrow about their request.

Jacob: Why have you done the evil of telling him you have a brother?

Reuben: The man asked us direct questions, saying, "Is your father still alive? Do you have another brother?" We answered him without knowing what he would require of us.

Judah: Let him go with us, Father; I will be a surety for him. From my hand shall you require him, and I promise to bring him back home. Send him with us to save Simeon and keep us, you and our younger ones from dying of hunger.

Jacob: If this be the case, then take him along with double the money required and the money you found in your sacks. Take also the best fruits of the land: a little balm, a little honey, spices, myrrh, nuts, and almonds to him. May God grant you mercy before the man. If I be bereaved of my children, I am forever bereaved.

They took all their father told them to take and departed to Egypt to get food.

When the brothers arrived in Egypt, Joseph saw Benjamin and was happy.

Joseph: Chief! Bring these men to the house, slay and make ready food, for they shall dine with me at noon.

Chief: Yes, lord, it will be done. Welcome, gentlemen, please come with me to the house of my master.

They became very afraid, and they began to debate amongst themselves.

Gad: Could it be because of the money?

Asher: I bet it was kept there that he may find us guilty and punish us.

Naphtali: *We are doomed!*

They saw the steward near the corner of the house.

Judah: *Sir, we were here another time to get food but, when we got home, we found our money back in our sacks. Please; we have brought it back with other money. Please, we do not know who put it in our sacks.*

Steward: *Peace be unto you. Do not be afraid, for God hath given you treasure in your sacks.*

He brought Simeon out to them and took them into the house of Joseph.

Chief: *Take your seats, gentlemen, my master will be with you shortly.*

Water was given to them to wash their feet. They prepared their gifts, laying them out before the arrival of Joseph.

Judah: *Check if our gifts are in good condition.*

Reuben: *Place them well, for he will soon be here.*

Joseph entered with his interpreter.

They brought the presents forward and bowed before him.

Reuben: *These presents are for you, sir.*

Joseph: *Thank you. How be you all?*

They responded that they were well.

Joseph: *How is your father? Is he still alive?*

They answered that he was alive and in good health. They bowed and made obeisance, and then Joseph lifted up his eyes and saw Benjamin, his brother from the same mother.

Joseph: *Is this your brother of whom ye spake?*

They all answered that he was.

Joseph: *God's grace and mercy be upon you, son.*

He noticed he was getting emotional, so he hurried to his chamber and wept there.

Naphtali: *Is everything okay with him?*

Asher: *Speak softly! He is fine. Stop talking!*

Joseph came back into the room and the table was set for them to eat. They sat down before him according to birthright, and all the men were surprised because of this. They drank and were merry with him.

Joseph called to the steward.

Steward: *My lord?*

Joseph: *Fill their sacks with food, as much as they can carry, and return their money unto them.*

Joseph also commanded in secret that his cup be kept in Benjamin's sack. He departed to his chamber and commanded they should be allowed to go home in the morning.

Joseph: *Steward! Come.*

Steward: *Yes, sir.*

Joseph: *Ride and overtake these people before they go too far, and ask them why they have done such a great evil in stealing my cup from me.*

The steward did as he was bid and overtook them.

Steward: *Why have you done this great evil of stealing from my master?*

They all responded, "Steal?"

Reuben: *God forbid we do such a thing! We even brought back the money that was left in our sacks the other time.*

Judah: *If thy master's gold or silver be found with any of us, let such a person be put to death and the rest of us made bondsmen.*

Steward: *And it shall be according to your words.*

Reuben: Put down your sacks, everyone, and open them for him to see.

They all did what Reuben said, and the cup was found in Benjamin's sack.

Asher: What!?

Naphtali: This is trouble.

Dan: How do we explain this to our father?

Benjamin: I swear, I know nothing about this. I am innocent!

They all tore at their clothes and returned to the city with the steward.

They arrived at Joseph's house.

Joseph: Why have you done this great evil?

Judah: We know not what to do or say to justify ourselves. Our iniquities have been found. Therefore, we all are servants unto you.

Joseph: That cannot be, because only the offender shall be punished. The rest of you can return to your father.

Judah: My lord, please let not your anger be against your servant, Benjamin, because you hold the same authority as Pharaoh. You asked us of our father and our brother, and we did not lie to you about them. We even told you about the one that died who is of the same mother with our youngest brother. If we return home without our brother, our father has told us his hairs will grow down to the grave and he will be forever bereaved. Please, if we return without our brother, our father shall behold us and die. The blame shall be upon me forever, because I stand in surety for the return of our Benjamin.

Joseph's eyes filled with tears.

Joseph: Everyone! Leave us alone.

The steward and other servants left, and Joseph began to cry out so loudly that all the Egyptians heard.

Joseph: I am Joseph, thy brother, whom ye sold to Egypt!

Benjamin: You are Joseph?

Joseph: Yes, I am.

They embraced each other and cried, shaking, on each other's shoulders.

Joseph: Is my father still alive?

They all answered that yes, he was.

Joseph: Blame yourselves not about anything that has happened, because God has sent me forth to preserve your lives.

They all wept.

Joseph: Go now unto my father and tell him I am still alive. Tell him that you all are to come into the land of Goshen, which is close to me, and there you shall remain while I continue to nourish you with good food. Tell him also of my glory in Egypt.

A report was taken to Pharaoh.

Guard: Sir, Joseph's brethren have come into Egypt.

Pharaoh stood up.

Pharaoh: Are you sure of these things which you speak of?

Guard: Yes, my lord.

Pharaoh was pleased to hear it.

Pharaoh: Take me there.

Pharaoh arrived, and the place and was happy with light and love.

Pharaoh: Joseph! Ye shall command all your family to move into Egypt, and they shall eat of the fatness of the land.

Reuben and his brothers returned home with the good news.

Reuben: Father! Father! Guess who we have found?

Jacob: Who?

Judah: Joseph! Joseph is alive and has sent for us all to move to Egypt!

Jacob: My son! My son is alive!

The father, with his son restored to him, was happy beyond bounds.

The family packed their things and made for Egypt with wagons given to them by Pharaoh. This marked the day that Jacob, whose name was also Israel, and his family moved into Egypt, and they became known as Israelites, according to Israel's name.

THE EXPERIENCES OF THE
ISRAELITES IN EGYPT

The Israelites lived and multiplied in the land of Egypt until the death of many that first entered into the city and the rise of a new generation. A new pharaoh came into power after the death of the former. The new ruler despised the Israelites, and the prophesy that was forgotten long ago came to pass, for they were made slaves by him in the land.

The horror and darkness grew greater as Pharaoh ordered the killing of all male children. In that same year did Jochebed, a Hebrew woman, conceive and give birth to a son. She tried to hide the babe to keep him from danger. She knew to keep him safe she must let him go, but she was filled with sadness and longed that it might not be so.

Jochebed: *Come, Miriam, let us get to the river bank where the daughter of Pharaoh's chambers are and put him there. God be with us! Pray we are lucky and she finds him.*

Miriam: *Yes, Mum, let us go.*

They put the child in a basket and took him to the river's edge. They placed his basket among the reeds and nudged it into the flow of the water. They prayed that Pharaoh's daughter would find the child and raise her. Miriam stood some distance from the basket and waited. And watched.

Pharaoh's daughter beckoned her maids to prepare for her bath in the river.

Pharaoh's daughter: *Hold my gown for me.*

The maid collected the gown. Pharaoh's daughter walked straight into the water to take her bath, her maids standing and waiting for the commands of their mistress. The basket floated among the reeds. She saw it and called one of her maids to fetch it.

Pharaoh's daughter: *What is this?*

She opened the basket to see what was inside, and she discovered a baby boy. He began to cry.

Maid 1: *A child! A fine one.*

Pharaoh's daughter: *He is so beautiful!*

Maid 2: *He is Hebrew.*

Pharaoh's daughter had compassion for the child and took him out of the basket.

Pharaoh's daughter: *It is true; he is one of the Hebrew's children.*

Miriam came out from her hiding place in the rushes.

Miriam: Shall I go and call a nurse of the Hebrew women to take care of him?

Pharaoh's daughter: Who are you? How long have you been observing?

Miriam: I am Miriam, a Hebrew. I can get you the best person to nurse him.

Pharaoh's daughter: Go and get her for me. Wait! No one hears about this!

Miriam: No one will.

Miriam went and called her mother to come take care of the child. Jochebed arrived at the palace.

Jochebed: Here I am, mistress.

Pharaoh's daughter: I hear you can take good care of the child for me.

Jochebed: Yes, I can.

Pharaoh's daughter: You shall take good care of him and return him to me as my own son.

Jochebed: I will do as you wish. Come, Miriam, let us go.

Pharaoh's daughter turned to her maids.

Pharaoh's daughter: Speak of this to nobody.

Maids: Yes, mistress.

Jochebed and Miriam took care of the child and returned him to Pharaoh's daughter when he was old enough.

Jochebed: Here is the boy, mistress. I cared for him as promised.

Pharaoh's daughter: Thank you. What shall I name this child? Hmmm, I shall call him Moses, because he was found by the water. His name is Moses.

Jochebed and Miriam left the child with Pharaoh's daughter and returned home, hiding their welling sadness.

Moses grew in the palace with Ramses, the son of Pharaoh, as his Hebrew brother.

As boys are wont to do, they perpetrated all manner of deeds, the terrible, the foolish, and sometimes the reasonable. They were known in the palace to be responsible for so many incidents, both good and bad, and Moses is always there to save them from trouble after getting them into it.

The Israelites labored and built all day under the unforgiving sun and unrelenting guards.

Guard: *Move it! You, over there!*

Guard 2: *Get your lazy self up and go back to work!*

The guards whipped the emaciated slaves and made them work even when their bones could not take any more.

Man 1: *No! He is dying! Stop whipping him.*

Man 2: *Help him up!*

Guard: *Get back!. Do not touch him.*

The guard flogged him once more, and the man died.

The suffering of the Israelites continued day in and day out with no sign of release or respite.

Moses was out one day when he ran into Miriam and her mother. They, of course, knew Moses, but Moses had no idea who they were of who he truly was.

Miriam: *Does he not know us still?*

Aaron: *He does not know who we are. He joins the guards every day to discipline us.*

Moses: *You! Lady, why are you always looking at me? Get back to work.*

He pushed them back to work. Miriam wept not because of what was done to her but because her own brother did it.

Jochebed: Miriam! It is going to be fine. He will remember us some day.

Moses always looked at his mother as though something about her was familiar, but he could not figure it out.

Miriam: I think we have to tell him.

Jochebed: If you do that, you will lead him to his death and us to our doom.

They wept and continued with their daily activities.

A few days later, Moses saw his mother again.

Moses: Lady! You again? I am going to punish you harshly this time around.

He raised his hand to beat her after pushing her away.

Miriam: I am your sister! You are Hebrew, not an Egyptian!

Moses froze, in shock. The whip dropped from his hand, and he ran away from them to Pharaoh's chamber.

Moses: How could this be? Can it be possible?

Ramses: Hey! Brother! I have some nice things to show you, but first let us go and see the complete structure of Anubis.

Moses hid his consternation and followed him in their usual playful manner.

MOSES BEGINS HIS JOURNEY

M oses could no longer lift his hands against any Israelite; he walked past them in pity, and they all wondered if all was well with him. His heart was troubled, so he decided to go to the camp of the Israelites at night to seek the truth.

Moses: Hello!

Jochebed: Welcome, my lord.

Moses: Where is your daughter?

Miriam came out of the house.

Moses: What do you mean by saying I am your brother and I am Hebrew?

Miriam: *You are indeed. You are my brother, and Jochebed is your mother, our mother.*

Jochebed: Yes! I am your mother. I gave birth to you when Pharaoh ordered the killing of every newborn male child in the Hebrew camp.

Moses: How then did I survive the killing?

Jochebed: I put you in a basket and told your sister to stay and watch over you until you were found by Pharaoh's daughter. She did find you and sought a Hebrew woman to take care of you, as she realized you were a Hebrew. Your sister then came to me to call me to do the job, which I did, and I gave you back to Pharaoh's daughter when you were weaned.

Moses wept, for he had done much evil to them without knowing they were his brethren. He embraced them and they consoled each other before he left for the palace of Pharaoh.

Moses went to his Egyptian mother.

Moses: *Mother! Why have you hidden the reality of my birth from me?*

She was shocked.

Pharaoh's daughter: What do you mean by this?

Moses: *I am not an Egyptian, and you have kept this truth from me.*

Pharaoh's daughter: *It is true, I found you floating in the river inside a basket when I went to take my bath. I knew you were Hebrew, but I loved you, so I took you and cared for you as my own child without allowing any harm to come to you.*

Moses wept.

Moses: *Why is this happening to me?*

He left her, disappointed and in tears.

Pharaoh's daughter: *Wait! Wait!*

Moses ignored her cries and fled to his own chamber. She was sad and afraid the boy might leave her for good but Moses did not.

Two days later, Moses was out at a worksite when he saw an Egyptian guard smiting a Hebrew.

Egyptian Guard: *Hey, you! Do those arms of yours work properly?*

Hebrew man: *Please, have mercy, please!*

Moses: *What has he done?*

Egyptian Guard: Master! He has refused to work properly the way he should. He is lazy.

Moses: What?

Moses checked around him and saw no one who could report his action. He slew the Egyptian.

Moses: You! Hurry and get out of here.

The Hebrew slave wasted no time in fleeing. Moses hid the body in the sand and fled himself.

The next day, Moses was taking a walk and saw to Hebrews fighting.

Moses: Stop! Why do you fight one another? What wrong has he done to you?

Hebrew man 1: What is your business in this? Who made you judge over us?

Hebrew man 2: Who made you prince and judge over us? Do you wish to slay us as you did the Egyptian?

Moses: What! Who told you this?

Moses became afraid and ran away to his chamber.

The matter reached Pharaoh's ears.

Pharaoh: Moses! Where is he? Guards, get Moses!

Moses, approaching the palace, heard the order of the king to get him. He quickly ran and fled the city to the land of Midian. There, he sat by a well.

Moses: I narrowly escaped death.

He was tired, so he tried to rest by the well. Seven daughters of the priest of the Midian approached the well to get water. They giggled behind their hands as they contemplated the sleeping boy.

Daughter 1: *What do you think of him? You are constantly looking at him.*

Daughter 2: *I think he likes you.*

Daughter 3: *How can you tell?*

The other four were also discussing Moses behind the three. They got to the well and began to fetch water to fill their troughs and water their father's flock.

Shepherd: *Get away from that well, you women of no value!*

Moses woke up from his sleep when he heard the shout of the shepherd.

Moses: *No! Let them stay and fetch in peace!*

Shepherd: *Of what concern is this matter to you?*

Moses: *It is of every concern to me.*

Shepherd: *Oh! You are Egyptian.*

Seeing that Moses was ready for a fight, the shepherd left them in peace and Moses helped them fetch the water.

Moses: *Bring your troughs closer; let me help you get the water you need.*

Daughters: *Thank you very much.*

Daughter 1: *We really appreciate your kind gesture.*

Daughter 7: *We shall tell of your goodness to our father.*

Moses: *Thank you very much. Please enjoy the day and be safe.*

They got back home to Jethro, their father.

Jethro: What! How come you have returned so soon?

Daughter 1: *Father, we met with an Egyptian by the well. He helped us with the water.*

Daughter 4: *He even saved us from the shepherd and his friends who tried to bully us.*

Jethro: *If that be the case, call unto me the Egyptian and let us eat bread together.*

Moses was invited to Jethro's house.

Jethro: *Welcome to my home. What is your name?*

Moses: *I am Moses.*

Jethro: *Welcome, Moses. My daughters told me of your kind gesture to them. Thank you. What can you tell me about yourself?*

Moses: *I am an Egyptian; I left my country because of something that has befallen me. I dwell by the well side because I have no place of my own to dwell.*

Jethro: *This day shall your problems be given a solution. If it pleases you, you shall continue to dwell with me in my house and no evil shall come to you.*

Moses: *Thank you very much for this which you have done.*

Jethro: *As a reward for the good which you have done, I have a gift for you.*

You! Call Zipporah.

Zipporah: *Father, here I am.*

Jethro held her by the wrist.

Jethro: *Here is my daughter, Zipporah, I give her to you as a wife.*

Moses: *Thank you very much for your kind deed.*

Moses dwelled with his wife, Zipporah, in the house of Jethro, and he was a happy man. He had a son named Gershom with Zipporah. He forgot about all that happened to him in Egypt and started a new life.

MOSES GOES BACK TO EGYPT

The Israelites remained in dire straits after Moses left Egypt; their situation was reaching new heights of horror.

In the palace, Pharaoh lay dying.

Physician: We have tried all we could, but his bones are too weak because of his age.

Ramses: Is there nothing else which could be done to save him?

Physician: We will continue to carry on.

Pharaoh died two days after and was mourned all over the land of Egypt.

At the Israelite camp, rumors and truths flew like sparrows.

Man 1: *I heard the king is dead.*

Lady 1: *It is no longer news. We await the next command from Ramses, who will be the next Pharaoh.*

The Israelites knew their suffering would continue without end, and they gathered together and cried unto God for a breakthrough. God heard their prayer and prepared the way.

At Midian, Moses moved with the flock of Jethro to the back side of the desert and came to Horeb, the mountain of God. Fire came upon a bush right in the presence of Moses, and the bush was not consumed. An angel of the Lord appeared to him amidst the burning bush.

Moses: *What is this? How does it happen that the bush is not consumed?*

The voice of God came to Moses from the burning bush.

God: *Moses! Moses!*

Moses: *Here am I.*

God: *Come not further. Pull off your shoe, for this is a holy ground.*

Moses: *Who are you?*

God: *I am the God of thy father, the God of Abraham, the God of Jacob.*

Moses hid his face in fear.

God: *I have seen the affliction of my people in Egypt and I have heard their cry. I have seen their oppression and I know their sorrows. I have come to deliver them from the hands of the Egyptians unto a land flowing with milk and honey. Now I will send you unto Pharaoh and you shall bring forth my children out of the land of Egypt. I will be with thee and upon this mountain you shall serve me when you bring the children of Israel out of the land of Egypt.*

Moses: What shall I say unto the Israelites when I get to them? Whom shall I tell them has sent me? What name would I mention when they ask?

God: I Am that I Am. Tell them "I Am" hath sent you to them. Go and gather the elders of Israel together and say to them, "The Lord God of your fathers, the God of Abraham, Isaac and Jacob appeared unto me saying I have seen the affliction of my people and I shall bring them out unto a land flowing with milk and honey." And they shall listen to you. Then you and the elders shall go unto Pharaoh and say to him, "The Lord God of the Hebrew hath met with us, now let us go, we beseech you three days' journey into the wilderness that we may sacrifice to the Lord our God." Know that Pharaoh will not let you go, but I will stretch out my hand and smite Egypt with my wonders. And when you shall go, you shall not go empty, for you shall find favor in the sight of the Egyptians.

Moses: They will not believe me if I say all these things. They will say the Lord has not appeared to me.

God: What do you have in thy hand?

Moses: A rod.

God: Cast it.

It changed into a serpent and Moses fled from it.

God: Stretch forth your hand and pick it up by the tail.

Moses picked it and it changed back into a rod.

God: This is a sign for you to show them that they may believe you. Put forth your hand into thy bosom.

Moses did so and leprosy was upon his hand when he brought it forth.

God: Put it back.

Moses obeyed and the hand was transformed back into flesh.

God: If they will not believe you after the first sign, they shall believe you after the second. If they don't, take water from the river and pour it upon dry land and it shall change to blood.

Moses: *But my Lord, I am not eloquent; I am slow in speech and of a slow tongue.*

God: *Who made the mouth of man? Who made the dumb and the deaf? Who made the seeing and the blind? Did not I? Now go and I will be with thy mouth and teach you what to say.*

Moses: *O my Lord, please, this is difficult.*

God became angry with Moses.

God: *Is Aaron the Levite not your brother? I know he can speak well. You shall go with him and he shall be your mouth. And you shall also take along with you always the rod in your hand as a sign.*

Moses returned to Jethro, his father in law.

Jethro: *Welcome, my son.*

Moses: *Thank you, Father. I have something to discuss with you.*

Jethro: *What could that be?*

Moses: *I have to go and do the bidding of God, for he has spoken to me. I must return to my brethren in Egypt and see whether they are alive.*

Jethro: *You are free to go in peace, my son.*

Moses was packing his things and thinking about those who sought him. God spoke in his heart.

God: *Why do you worry about those who want you dead? They are all dead that sought your life.*

Moses then freely took his wife, son and his rod and they traveled down to the land of Egypt.

God: *Moses! See that you do all the wonders which I have put in your hands* *when you get to Egypt. I will harden his heart that he will not let you go. Then you shall say to him, "Thou saith the Lord, Israel is my son, even my firstborn. I say to you, let them go that they may serve me, and if you refuse to let them go, I will slay thy son, even thy firstborn."*

The Lord also spoke with Aaron.

God: *Aaron!*

Aaron: *Here I am.*

God: *I am the God of your father Abraham, Isaac and Jacob. Go now to the wilderness and meet Moses.*

Aaron departed to the wilderness and found Moses there.

Aaron: *Moses!*

Moses: *Aaron!*

They embraced and kissed each other. Moses told him about the instructions God had given to him and how they were to work together to do His will. They left and gathered together all the elders of the children of Israel.

Aaron spoke the words of Moses, which he got from God.

Elders: *How are we to believe you?*

Aaron: *"I Am" has sent me. The God of your fathers, Abraham, Isaac, and Jacob.*

Moses cast his rod and did the wonders which God had put in his hands, and they believed him.

Aaron: *God has heard our cry and is ready to deliver us from the hand of Pharaoh and from Egypt to the land that flows with milk and honey.*

The Israelites felt relieved because they believed they would soon be free. They bowed their heads and worshipped God.

. . .

Moses and Aaron went before Pharaoh.

Pharaoh (Ramses): Moses! Brother, where have you been? I tried to find you, to bring you back when Father died, but I had no idea where you had gone.

Moses: Ramses!

They hugged and Ramses pronounced Moses a Prince of Egypt.

Moses: I have come to you with words from God. Saith the Lord, "Let my people go that they may serve me."

Pharaoh: What are you talking about, Moses? We have it all, now! We can be together like before! What God are you talking about?

Moses: He is "I Am."

Pharaoh: I do not know the Lord you speak of. Who is he that I should obey him? I will not obey him, and I will not let the people of Israel go, either. The land has increased and so has the work of the land. Who will do the work of the Israelites if I let them go?

Moses: The Lord said, "Let my people go that they may serve me."

Pharaoh: I shall make their burden greater for this reason. The officers shall no longer give them straw to make bricks. They will have to get it themselves.

PHARAOH'S STUBBORNNESS AND ITS CONSEQUENCES

The pain upon the people of Israel increased, and they began to protest in earnest. Officers of the children of Israel went unto Pharaoh.

Officer: Why have you chosen to deal with us in this manner? There is no straw given to us and your guards request us to make bricks. They beat us, yet they give not to us straws.

Pharaoh: Why do you request to go and serve your God and make sacrifices unto him? Straw shall no longer be given unto you. You shall go in search of it yourselves. Depart from me now and get back to work.

The officers departed from Pharaoh but they met Moses and Aaron on their way out of Pharaoh's palace.

Officers: *May God judge you, for you have increased our burden and made our lives more miserable still.*

Moses was confused about the matter and went to inquire of the Lord.

Moses: *God, why have sent me? Why have you chosen to deal with these people in this evil manner? My presence has brought more misfortune, and you have not delivered them.*

God: *Moses! Now shall you see what I shall do with Pharaoh, for with a strong hand shall he let the people of Israel go. Go to the children of Israel and say to them, "I am the Lord, I appeared unto Abraham, Isaac, and Jacob by the name of God Almighty, but by my name Jehovah they know me not. I have established my covenant with them to give them the land of Canaan, the land of their pilgrimage, wherein they are strangers. I have heard their cry and I will deliver them."*

Moses departed from the presence of the Lord and went to the people of Israel, but they believe him not, even after he told them what the Lord had said unto him.

God spoke with Moses and again told him to go and speak unto Pharaoh that he may let his people go.

Moses: *Behold, the children of Israel have not listened to me. How then shall Pharaoh listen? To me, of an uncircumcised lip?*

God: *Moses! I have made you a god to Pharaoh and Aaron your brother shall be your prophet. You shall speak all that I told you, and Aaron your brother shall speak to Pharaoh to let the children of Israel out of his hands. Behold, I will harden Pharaoh's heart and I will multiply my signs and wonders in the land of Egypt. The Egyptians shall know that I am the Lord when I stretch forth my hand upon Egypt, for Pharaoh will not harken unto you until I stretch forth my hand upon Egypt. When Pharaoh shall demand a miracle* *from you, tell your brother Aaron to cast thy rod and it shall become a serpent.*

Moses and Aaron did as the Lord commanded and went to see Pharaoh.

Moses: Pharaoh! "Let my people go that they may worship me," said the Lord!

Pharaoh: Moses, you are here again. When will you give up on this impossible mission of yours? What sign have you from your Lord that sent you?

Moses told Aaron to cast the rod. Aaron did according to Moses and the rod became a snake. Pharaoh laughed out loud.

Pharaoh: You call this a sign from your Lord. Even my magician can do this. Call the magician.

The magicians arrived immediately they casted their rods and they became snakes, too. But Moses's snake swallowed all the snakes. Aaron picked it up by the tail and it changed back to the rod. Pharaoh was shocked but refused to bend, because he was hard hearted.

Pharaoh: It is just a simple trick, as you can see. Even my magicians did it. Moses! I am not letting your people go. Depart from me.

Moses and Aaron departed from the presence of Pharaoh.

God spoke to Moses again.

God: Moses, get to Pharaoh in the morning, when he is going to the water, and stand by the river bank. Wait for him there. Take thy rod with you and say to him, "The Lord God of the Hebrews hath sent me unto thee, saying, let my people go, that they may serve me in the wilderness."

Moses departed to see Pharaoh just as instructed.

Moses: Pharaoh! Let my people go that they may serve me, said the Lord God of the Hebrews.

Pharaoh: Moses! It is never going to happen.

Moses: And this shall be a sign for you to know the Lord has sent me.

He told Aaron to smite the river with the rod. He did, and it changed into blood. The fish began to die.

Pharaoh: Impressive. Guard! Get me the magicians.

Magicians: Here we are, Master.

Pharaoh: Show him how cheap his tricks are.

Magicians: This man has failed to repent; let us show him what we can do, too.

They did some incantation and the water in the bowl they were holding changed to blood.

Pharaoh: As you can see, your tricks are cheap. Moses! I will not let your people go.

Pharaoh, his guards and the magicians left the river's edge. Within days, the river began to stink because of the dead fish floating bloated on its still-ruddy surface. The Egyptians had to dig around the river before they could get water to drink. For seven days, the Egyptians suffered from the lack of water.

The Lord spoke to Moses again.

God: Moses! Go unto pharaoh and say to him, "Thus saith the Lord, let my people go that they may serve me and if you refuse, I shall smite your borders with frogs."

Moses went again with his brother Aaron to see Pharaoh. Pharaoh was seated on his throne when they arrived at the palace to see him.

Moses: Pharaoh! Thus saith the Lord, "Let my people go that they may serve me and if you refuse, I shall smite your borders with frogs. Your river shall bring forth frogs abundantly. It shall be a great disaster to your kingdom."

Pharaoh laughed.

Pharaoh: Moses! I will not let the Israelites go.

God then spake to Moses again.

God: *Moses! Say unto Aaron to stretch forth the rod in his hand over the streams, over the rivers, and over the ponds and cause frogs to come up upon the land of Egypt.*

Moses did as instructed by God, and the land of Egypt was filled with frogs, except for the camp of the Israelites.

Pharaoh, looking confused and amazed, called for his magicians.

Magicians: *Yes, sir?*

Pharaoh: *Show unto this man you can do the same thing as his Lord and make the frogs depart this place!*

Magicians: *Yes, sir!*

They did some incantations and frogs still came out of the rivers, ponds and streams upon the land of Egypt. They could not cause it to stop.

Pharaoh: *Moses! I will not let them go!*

He departed to his chamber as everyone in the palace sought a place to hide themselves from the frogs, but they found none.

Moses and Aaron left the palace and departed to the camp of the Israelites.

After days of the affliction with frogs, Pharaoh was seated in his palace, confused about what to do.

Pharaoh's wife: *You have to do something about this, because the people are complaining.*

Counselor: *My lord! Behold the people are crying and beginning to lose faith in your reign. Something has to be done about this.*

Pharaoh uttered no words to anyone.

Pharaoh: *Guards! Get to the camp of the Israelites and tell Moses and Aaron to come forth to the palace so I could have a word with them.*

Guards: *Yes, sir.*

They departed to the camp of the Israelites to call Moses and Aaron. At the camp of the Israelites, people began to murmur at the sight of the guards. What did they want? Why were they here? Had they come to destroy us?

They came unto Moses and Aaron.

Guard: *Moses! Pharaoh would like to have a word with you and Aaron.*

Moses: *We will be there.*

They departed to the palace and Moses and Aaron followed.

Pharaoh: *Moses! I have decided to let your people go. Entreat your Lord to get rid of these frogs from the land and I shall let the people go.*

Moses: *Glory be to God. When do you wish for this to happen?*

Pharaoh: *Tomorrow.*

Moses: *So be it.*

They departed from the palace while Pharaoh remained on his throne looking like a king that has just lost a battle.

At the camp of the Israelites, Moses and Aaron arrived with good news.

Moses: *Hear ye, my people! Pharaoh has decided to let us go. By this time tomorrow we will be on our way out of Egypt.*

The people screamed and rejoiced because their days of suffering were nigh at an end. Moses went to a quiet place to seek the face of

God. He prayed to God to rid the land of Egypt of the frogs and God did according to what he requested.

Pharaoh was moving along a corridor of the palace.

Pharaoh: *What? They are dying! They are dying!*

All the frogs died until none remained in the land. Pharaoh was happy as he moved around the palace, laughing. The frogs were heaped together and because of it, the land began to smell terrible.

Moses: *Pharaoh! The frogs are gone from your land. Now let my people go that we may sacrifice to our Lord in the wilderness.*

Pharaoh: *(He laughed) I am free of the affliction your Lord brought upon my land. Why then should I let your people go? Moses! It is not possible.*

Moses and Aaron were disappointed, but the Lord spoke to Moses concerning what to do.

God: *Moses! Speak to Aaron to stretch out the rod in his hands and smite the dust of the Earth.*

Moses did as instructed and all the dust in the land became lice. Pharaoh looked about, panicking.

Pharaoh: *Get the magicians, now! I will show you there is nothing your Lord can do that my magicians cannot do easily! Seeing the situation, the magicians already understood why Pharaoh had called them. They immediately began incantations to bring forth lice, but nothing worked.*

Pharaoh: *What is happening?*

Magicians: *This is beyond our skills, sir. This is the finger of God.*

Pharaoh: *What?! Get away from me, you worthless people.*

They departed from Pharaoh so he might not smite them in his anger.

Pharaoh: *Yet I will not let them go!!!!!*

Moses and Aaron departed to the camp of the Israelites. They are back! They are back, the people of the land shouted. However, the look on the faces of Moses and Aaron passed a clear message.

People: *Pharaoh has deceived us.*

They returned to their tents, once more dispirited.

God spoke to Moses again.

God: *Moses! Rise up in the morning and stand before Pharaoh, for he'll come to water. Say to him, "Thus saith the Lord, let my people go that they may serve me else I will send upon you and your servants swarms of flies and it shall be everywhere except the land of Goshen where the Israelites dwell, and I shall put division between my people and your people."*

Moses did as the Lord commanded him, but Pharaoh was stone-hearted and he refused to let them go. And there were flies everywhere in the camp of the Egyptians.

Pharaoh called one of his guards.

Pharaoh: *Go to the camp of the Israelites and call to me Moses and Aaron.*

The guard departed while Pharaoh sat on his throne of flies and waited for his return. Moses and Aaron came to the palace after some hours.

Pharaoh: *Moses! Go and sacrifice to your God in the land. You have my permission.*

Moses: *Pharaoh! We cannot sacrifice in the land of Egypt, because we will also sacrifice the abomination of Egypt. This would be a serious sin in the sight of your people and they will be sure to stone us to death. We will go three days into the wilderness and sacrifice unto our God as he has commanded us.*

Pharaoh: *If that be the case, then I shall let you go, but before I do that, pray to your God for me that the land may be free from all the flies infesting it.*

Moses: *I shall pray to our Lord for you, but do not deal deceitfully with us* anymore. *The swarm of flies shall depart from you and your servant tomorrow.*

Moses and Aaron departed from Pharaoh, and Moses went into a quiet place and prayed to God and the Lord did according to the demand of Moses.

The next day, the buzzing swarms swirled away from the land of Egypt. But Pharaoh's heart was still hardened.

Moses: *Pharaoh! Now let us go.*

Pharaoh: *Never! I will not let them go.*

The Lord kept visiting the land of Egypt with more plagues. The hand of the Lord was upon the cattle, horses, asses, camels, oxen and sheep of the Egyptians and there was murrain, for all the animals died, yet Pharaoh refused to let the people of Israel go.

God: *Moses! Take a handful of ashes and sprinkle it toward the heavens in the sight of Pharaoh and they shall be visited with boils, both men and beasts.*

Moses did as God told him; he got ashes from the furnace and sprinkled it and boils sprouted upon the people of Egypt. The magicians could not stand before Pharaoh because they were afflicted with boils, too, yet Pharaoh refused to let the people of Israel go.

The Lord spoke to Moses again that he shall bring down hail upon the land and every man should gather their cattle to their houses from the fields. All the Israelites and Egyptians who had regard for the word of God did what the Lord commanded them, and the Lord smote the land with a hail of fire and destroyed the herbs of the fields, beasts and humans.

Pharaoh: *I cannot take this anymore! You, over there! Go to Goshen and call to me Moses and Aaron.*

Moses and Aaron arrived the palace.

Pharaoh: I deceive you not anymore; pray to your God for me to take away these abominations from my land and I shall let you go.

Moses: I shall stretch forth my hand and your city shall be free, but I know you will not yet repent, despite what has been taken from you.

Moses left the palace of pharaoh and did as promised. The rain, thunder, and hail stopped, but Pharaoh's heart was hardened and he refused to let them go.

God spoke with Moses again to go to Pharaoh and tell him to let his people go, else he will visit the land with locusts.

Moses: Pharaoh! Thus said the Lord God of the Hebrews, "How long will you refuse to humble yourself before me? Let my people go, that they may serve me, else by tomorrow, I will visit your land with locusts!"

Pharaoh: How long shall you remain stiff-necked? For I will not let you and your people go.

Moses and Aaron departed from the palace. Some of Pharaoh's servants gathered unto him to advise him.

Servant: My lord, this man and his God have brought many things upon us already. Let them go that they may serve their God and we may be free before the worst befall us.

Pharaoh listened to them and demanded his servant call Moses and Aaron back to the palace.

Pharaoh: Who are the people that shall go from Egypt to make sacrifices unto your God?

Moses: We will go with our young, our old, our sons, our daughters, our flocks and our herds to hold a feast unto the Lord.

Pharaoh: No! Only the men shall go and make a feast unto your Lord, while the others will stay.

Moses: We all will leave! No one will stay behind, not even our cattle. That is the command of our God.

Pharaoh: Then no one shall leave. You will all stay behind and serve in the land of Egypt.

Moses left his presence and God spoke with him.

God: Moses! Stretch your rod over the land of Egypt for the locusts to come upon the land.

Moses did as instructed, and the Lord brought the east wind upon the land of Egypt all night, and the wind brought locusts all over the land by morning. The swarms of locusts were so dense that the land became as night, for they covered the whole of it. They consumed all the flora of the Egyptians, and nothing green was left behind.

Pharaoh's servants came to him to advise him.

Servant: My lord, I do not see victory of the Egyptians, because their Lord is strongly behind them. We have nothing left in the land that has a green color. Please let them go!

Pharaoh remained quiet for some minutes, then ordered his servants to call Moses and Aaron to the palace. The guards left while they all waited for the arrival of Moses and Aaron. Moses and Aaron arrived at the palace with the guards after some hours. Pharaoh looked defeated.

Pharaoh: Moses! Behold! I have sinned against you and the Lord your God. Please, pray to your God to take away this plague from me once more. I shall keep to my promise this time and let you and your people go.

Moses left with Aaron.

Pharaoh: Moses! Moses! Moses!

Moses left to pray to the Lord concerning that which Pharaoh said and the Lord did according to his request by taking away the locusts with wind into the Red Sea.

And when pharaoh saw that the locusts were taken away, his heart became harder and he said to himself, "I will never let them go."

The Lord spoke with Moses again.

God: Moses! Stretch forth thy hand toward the heavens and a thick darkness will be upon the land, but there will be light in the camp of the Israelites.

Moses did according to the Lord and there came upon the land of Egypt a blanket of dark.

In the house of an Egyptian, a small boy was crying.

Boy: Mama, where are you, I cannot see anything!

Mother: I can hear you, where are you?

The darkness brought confusion to the land, which was accompanied by a grave silence. Pharaoh sent for Moses.

Pharaoh: Moses! I have had enough of these things. Go and serve the Lord your God. Go with everyone but let your flocks and your herds stay behind.

Moses: We will go, but you shall also give us sacrifices and burnt offerings that we may sacrifice unto the Lord our God and none of our belongings shall remain behind. Even our cattle and hoof shall leave with us into the wilderness.

Pharaoh rose up in anger.

Pharaoh: What!? Get away from me and never shall you come before me again for the day you see my face again, you shall die.

Moses: Thou have spoken well. I will go away from you and will not see your face anymore.

Moses returned to the camp of the Israelites and the Lord spoke unto him.

God: Moses! One more plague will I now bring upon Egypt. Speak to every man to borrow from his neighbor jewels of silver and jewels of gold, and I shall grant the favor in the sight of the Egyptians.

Moses: Yes, my Lord.

Moses called Aaron.

Moses: *Aaron gather the people, for the Lord has spoken.*

Aaron did as he said and Moses came to address them all.

Moses: *The day of our freedom is here. Go ye every man, borrow from your neighbors jewels of silver and gold, for this is the commandment of the Lord. You shall not be afraid, for the Lord shall grant you favor in the sight of the Egyptians.*

They departed and did according to what Moses told them. Pharaoh's servants and the people of Egypt began to see Moses as a great man. They respected him, and the hand of the Lord was upon them that they favor the Israelites.

Moses gathered them once again.

Moses: *At midnight will the Lord visit the land of Egypt with the angel of death, and there shall be weeping all over the land, for all firstborn of the land of Egypt shall be taken away from them. Both the firstborn of humans and of all animals. And there shall be a great cry throughout the land of Egypt. On the tenth day of this month, shall every man take a lamb according to the house of his father. The lamb shall be without blemish and it shall be a male of the first year. On the fourteenth day he shall kill it in the evening and use the blood as a sign upon his house door post, for when the angel of death shall pass by, it shall be a sign to differentiate the house of the Egyptians from the house of the Israelites. The meat shall be roasted with fire and eaten with unleavened bread and with bitter herbs.*

And it came to pass that the night came and the angel of death visited Egypt and there was great cry across the land. The Egyptians cried and began to demand that the Israelites leave immediately.

Pharaoh sat on the floor with his lifeless son in his arms, weeping without anyone to console him, for everyone wept and mourned their own losses. He took him to the hand of the god in his palace, but nothing could be done. Then he called for Moses.

Moses arrived at the palace.

Moses: Ramses!

Pharaoh: Say nothing. Just take all your things and leave.

He turned his face away from Moses and Moses left the palace to return to his people. They all gathered waiting to hear what Moses has to say to them.

Moses: Let all men go into their tents, pack their properties and their families, for it is time to leave Egypt. There was joy and songs of joy all through the land as the Israelites packed their properties and started the journey out of the land that had so oppressed them.

The counselor came to Pharaoh.

Counselor: Sir, will you let them go despite all the evil they have done in the land? Let us chase after them take revenge and slay every one of them.

Pharaoh's heart was hardened once more.

Pharaoh: Guards! Gather the armies and the chariots. I shall have my revenge on the Israelites.

He went into the room to brace himself for war.

Chief of Armies: Sir! Your chariot is ready and the armies are ready for war.

Pharaoh entered his chariot and they began to chase after the Israelites. The Israelites were on their way when they noticed a great haboob rising from behind them because of Pharaoh's horses.

Israelites: Moses! Look, the Egyptians are after us.

The Israelites began to run, but God intervened and shielded them with a pillar of cloud during the day so that the Egyptians could not get to them and shielded them with pillar of fire at night. After chasing them for days, the Israelites arrived the Red Sea, and there was nowhere to turn.

Israelites: Moses! Moses! Look, they are upon us. Shall you look at us till we perish?

Moses prayed to God.

God: Moses! Stretch forth thy rod to the sea and it shall give way.

Moses did according to what God said and the sea gave way for the Israelites. They rejoiced and began to run through before the Egyptians could get to them.

Pharaoh's heart was still hardened so that he commanded his armies to chase after them through the sea.

God spoke to Moses again.

God: Moses! Now that every Israelite has crossed, stretch forth your rod toward the sea and it will flow against the Egyptians.

Moses obeyed and all the Egyptian armies perished right before the eyes of the Israelites. They crossed into the promised land, their children safe, their flocks intact, their goods and carriages undamaged. Moses stood fast against great evil and resistance, trusting in God, who delivered him and his people to freedom self-governance

CONCLUSION AND SIGNIFICANCE OF THE STORY

M ost people are familiar with the story of Joseph and his coat of many colors, and the tale of the Israelites' experience in Egypt. Few, however, realize the importance of these stories when it comes to God's ability to make anything happen for his chosen people. Also, the significance of these stories on the subjects of evangelism and obedience cannot be overemphasized. The brothers of Joseph did not believe his dream, but their unbelief would not stop God from carrying out what he planned. In the same manner, the Egyptians did not recognize the God of Israel; they could not imagine there was any other deity higher than those they served!

The Egyptians did not believe they were on the wrong path until the Lord sent Moses back to Pharaoh. The Egyptians worshipped idols and pagan gods of the water and sky, and snakes and other animal deities, but God of Israel forced them to recognize his sovereign power. God afflicted the Egyptians with ten plagues; each of the plagues was directed against the false gods they served. Each plague proved to the Egyptians (and other worshipers of idols in the world) that these false gods and goddesses are powerless.

. . .

The ten plagues directed to the Egyptians were not only meant to scare them, but to introduce them to the living God of Israel. Moreover, each time Pharaoh's heart was hardened and he refused to let the Israelites go gave God an opportunity to demonstrate his power, as he sent another shocking plague.

Obedience is the key to being at peace with God! Our obedience to God is very important; our sins create the chance for God to demonstrate his power in another dimension. He commanded Moses and Aaron to go before Pharaoh, and they never refused, obeying him even as they knew Pharaoh was full of deception. If they had refused, they themselves would have faced the fearsome power of God. Regardless, when one will not permit his heart to be moved by the word of God, it means his heart is hardened as was Pharaoh's, and even as God will forgive previous sins, engaging purposely with another sin will certainly attract greater destruction.

This story shows us how unwise it is to wait until you experience the worst before you listen to the word of God and obey his commandments. Don't wait until you are on the brink of losing everything that matters to you, including your loved ones. God wants us to pass our knowledge of him to the whole world, to the places and people where and to whom he remains unknown or has not been accepted. He used Moses to tell the people of Egypt about his omniscience and omnipotence; now he wants us to be the Moses of our time and bring his word to those who know not of him, so that all can live in the blessed state of the promised land.

ABOUT THE AUTHOR

James Taiwo is the founder and senior pastor of World Outreach Evangelical Ministry in New York City. He holds a Doctor of Theology degree and a Master of Science Degree in Environmental Engineering. A practicing civil and environmental engineer and preacher, James also plays saxophone and is an avid blogger. With the aim of diversifying the gospel to adapt to the fast-changing technology of our day, he is the publisher of Trumpet Media Ministries and author of several books, including *Bible Application Lessons and Prayers*, *Book of Prayers*, *Who Was Jesus Really?*, *Pinnacle of Compassion*, *Christian Principle Guides*, and *Roadmap to Success*. James lives in New York City with his wife and children.

CONNECT WITH THE AUTHOR

Please add your honest, positive reviews of this book online. Rate this book five stars now at
http://bit.ly/bookofegypt

Sign up for new book alert from the author at
www.bit.ly/bookalertme

Visit the author's website at
www.jamestaiwo.com

Connect with the author on social media

f facebook.com/jamestaiwoJT

🐦 twitter.com/theJamesTaiwo

a amazon.com/author/jamestaiwo

www.ingramcontent.com/pod-product-compliance
Lightning Source LLC
Chambersburg PA
CBHW060533030426
42337CB00021B/4238